LADYBIRD HISTORIES

The Great Fire of London

History consultant: Philip Parker

LADYBIRD BOOKS

UK | USA | Canada | Ireland | Australia
India | New Zealand | South Africa

Ladybird Books is part of the Penguin Random House group of companies
whose addresses can be found at global.penguinrandomhouse.com.

www.penguin.co.uk
www.puffin.co.uk
www.ladybird.co.uk

Penguin
Random House
UK

First published 2016
001

Printed in China

A CIP catalogue record for this book is available from the British Library

ISBN 978–0–241–24821–8

All correspondence to:
Ladybird Books
Penguin Random House Children's
80 Strand, London WC2R 0RL

Penguin Random House is committed to a
sustainable future for our business, our readers
and our planet. This book is made from Forest
Stewardship Council® certified paper.

LADYBIRD HISTORIES

The Great Fire of London

Written by Chris Baker
Main illustrations by Roger Wade Walker
Cartoon illustrations by Clive Goodyer

Contents

Introduction

On Sunday 2 September 1666, a fire started in a baker's shop in London. The baker's shop was in Pudding Lane, but the fire spread quickly to cover a large area of London in just a few days. No one could stop this fire before it burned down most of central London. It became known as the Great Fire of London, and this is its story.

How did the fire spread?

The fire burned until late on Wednesday 5 September. It affected a large area in the centre of London and the flames spread beyond the city wall to the west of the city.

Sunday 2 September
• The fire started at a bakery in Pudding Lane.

Monday 3 September
• The fire spread north and west, but the River Thames stopped it to the south.

Tuesday 4 September and Wednesday 5 September
• The flames crossed Cheapside and destroyed St Paul's Cathedral.

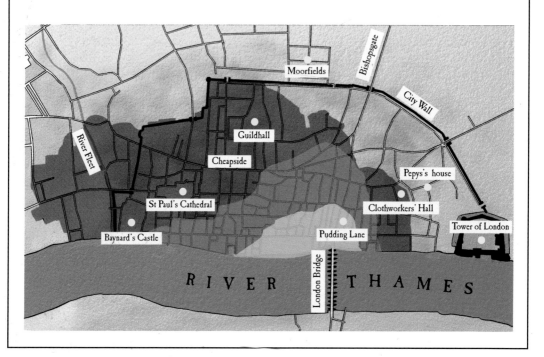

London before the fire

In 1666, London was a crowded city. It had narrow streets, and the upstairs parts of the buildings on each side were so close they almost touched each other. Most buildings were made of wood and plaster. People often lived in the building where they worked, even if their work was dangerous or messy. There was a lot of rubbish in the streets. The fleas on the rats that lived in the rubbish had caused an outbreak of plague in 1665. The air was smoky from the many fires people needed to heat their homes and cook their food.

The narrow streets of London were tightly packed with buildings.

Firefighting in 1666

People needed coal fires to heat their buildings and candles to light them. Many people needed fires for their work. House fires often started by accident. If a fire started, everyone nearby was supposed to come out and help. People would throw water on the fire with buckets or scoops, or use 'squirts', which were like big water pistols. Thatched roofs had been banned in the city back in 1212, but there were not many other rules to keep people safe and there was no fire brigade.

Firefighting equipment

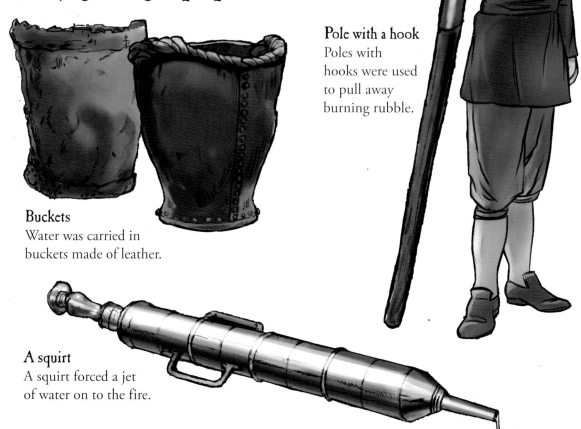

Pole with a hook
Poles with hooks were used to pull away burning rubble.

Buckets
Water was carried in buckets made of leather.

A squirt
A squirt forced a jet of water on to the fire.

An early fire engine

The top of the pipe could be angled towards the fire.

Water was stored in the large tub and pumped out by hand.

Our reporter, Samuel Pepys

Samuel Pepys worked in London at the time of the Great Fire, helping to organize the Royal Navy. His job meant that he knew many important people of the time, including the king. Samuel wrote a diary over a period of about ten years (1660–1669). During that time, he wrote about sixteen fires, including the Great Fire.

Sunday 2 September 1666

It had been a long, hot summer, so everything was dry. The buildings around Pudding Lane were mostly made of wood. Some of them were used to store wood, rope, oil and tar: all things that burned quickly and easily. These factors helped the fire to spread even more quickly.

A baker's shop contained many fire hazards.

This baker's shop shows how easy it might have been for a fire to start and take hold. Flammable objects such as bundles of dry straw and oil spills on the floor are dangerously close to the heat of the baker's oven.

Red-hot oven

Bundles of straw

Oil spill

The fire starts

Thomas Farriner and his daughter Hanna were bakers who lived above their bakery in Pudding Lane. Everything seemed normal when Hanna checked the oven before she went to bed. But at about 1 a.m. on Sunday 2 September the Farriners were woken by thick smoke. Their bakery was on fire and they were trapped upstairs! They had to climb out of a window and escape along the gutter to their neighbour's house.

The city is on fire – go back to bed!

At about 3 a.m., Samuel Pepys was woken up by his servants to see the fire. But he decided it was too far away to be a danger to his house, so he went back to bed.

Hanna had to escape from the upper floor.

The fire spreads

The Farriners and their neighbours couldn't put the fire out. Early on Sunday morning, someone sent for the Lord Mayor, Thomas Bloodworth, to ask permission to make firebreaks. The idea was to make gaps between the buildings that the fire couldn't cross. Everything left inside the firebreaks might be burned up, but after that the fire would go out. To make firebreaks they had to pull down the buildings near the edge of the fire, and take the rubble away. Destroying these buildings on purpose might save many other buildings.

Poles were used to pull down houses.

Samuel goes to see

On Sunday morning, Samuel Pepys heard that the fire had already burned down around 300 houses. He got up and went to see. The fire had started near the north bank of the River Thames. It could not cross the Thames, and people were escaping on to the river by boat. Samuel saw the fire was really bad now.

Government in London

King Charles II and Parliament were based in London. But neither the king nor Parliament ran the city.

The Lord Mayor of London, Thomas Bloodworth, was in charge – he was elected by the guilds. Each guild was an organization of tradesmen, such as butchers, bakers or bricklayers.

A chance lost?

The Lord Mayor came to see the fire. But he wanted the approval of the owner of each building before ordering it to be pulled down. He was criticized for wasting time and allowing the fire to spread further. There was a very strong wind, and this was blowing the fire along quickly.

Samuel Pepys took the Lord Mayor an order from the king – pull down houses without waiting for permission! But the Lord Mayor told Samuel: 'People will not obey me. I have been pulling down houses, but the fire overtakes us faster than we can do it.'

Disorganization

Instead of fighting the fire, people were busy trying to pack up their belongings and get them to safety. Samuel Pepys noticed that 'the streets and the highways are crowded with people running and riding, and getting of carts . . . to fetch away things.'

To add to the chaos, people who owned carts headed to London. Some of them wanted to help, but others hoped to make a lot of money by charging people to take their things to safety. Some people charged very high prices for the use of their carts – thousands of pounds in today's money – and there were stories that some people who were offering to help carry things were actually stealing them.

The roads were jammed with carts trying to get in and out of the city. This all added to the growing difficulties of fighting the fire. The authorities tried to ban carts, but many people ignored the ban.

Samuel packs

Samuel invited his friend Tom Hater to stay with them and bring his things – Tom's house was already on fire. But then Tom and Samuel heard the news that the fire was still spreading. Samuel decided he had better send some of his own things away. 'Which I did riding myself in my night-gown in the cart.'

The streets were blocked as people loaded their belongings on to carts.

The Duke of York takes charge

The spread of the fire by Sunday night

Pudding Lane

By Sunday night, Samuel Pepys wrote: 'we saw the fire as only one entire arch . . . of above a mile long: it made me weep to see it.' He added that it was: 'a most horrid malicious bloody flame, not like the fine flame of an ordinary fire. The churches, houses, and all on fire and flaming at once; and a horrid noise the flames made, and the cracking of houses at their ruins.'

Soldiers helped to organize and coordinate firefighting.

The Duke of York

On Monday 3 September, King Charles put his brother James, the Duke of York, in charge. James was an admiral and an experienced leader. He quickly set up command posts around the edge of the fire, and began making firebreaks. He got the king to promise that no one would be punished for destroying buildings to make firebreaks. The fear of punishment had slowed down work before. James himself rode back and forth between the command posts, encouraging people and reassuring everyone.

Refugees and rumours

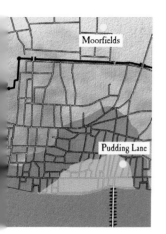

By Monday afternoon, the fire was so large and so fierce that the flames could be seen from Oxford, around 100 kilometres away. People began to flee to safety outside the city, camping on open ground at Moorfields, Hampstead and Finsbury Hill. Some people would have to stay there for many months. Back in the city, disorder became so widespread that the authorities struggled to keep it under control.

Many people left the city to escape the fire.

Samuel and the duke

Samuel spent most of the day packing up the rest of his things. But the Duke of York came to see him, and Samuel wrote approvingly that the duke 'did ride with his guard up and down the City, to keep all quiet'. Perhaps people would calm down if they realized that the duke was getting everything organized.

Rumours

False rumours began to spread that the fire was the work of foreign spies, and sadly this led to random attacks on foreigners. A Dutch baker was thrown into jail, and the Duke of York's soldiers had to save a French man from being beaten up by a mob. Another man, from the Portuguese Embassy, was attacked because people saw he was foreign and wrongly thought he was starting fires.

Foreigners were unfairly attacked.

Samuel stays put

Having packed up all his things, Samuel and his wife had an uncomfortable night, sleeping at Samuel's office: 'At night lay down a little upon a quilt in the office, all my own things being packed up or gone.' All they had to eat were 'the remains of yesterday's dinner, having no fire [to cook anything with] nor dishes'.

Tuesday 4 September – the worst day

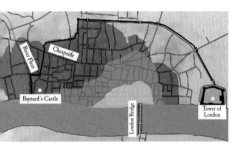

The Duke of York had hoped to stop the fire at the River Fleet, but the wind was so strong that it carried sparks across the river. When buildings on the other bank caught fire, the duke's men had to run for safety. The wind also drew the fire across Cheapside, the city's widest road. Cheapside should have formed a natural firebreak and a more organized strategy here might have stopped the blaze. But the fire was now so big and so hot that it could spread against the direction of the wind as well as downwind.

The flames spread as far south as the River Thames.

London Bridge

Grand buildings on fire

The fire burned down many famous buildings, including the Royal Palace of Baynard's Castle. The flames in the Grocers' Guild building were so hot that the grocers' treasure was found melted in the ruins. Even the king moved his personal goods. The flames were only a few hundred metres from the Tower of London, where gunpowder was stored.

Samuel fights the fire

Samuel sent all his workmen to make a firebreak, to try to save his office and its important papers. He also buried some possessions like wine and a Parmesan cheese – very valuable in those days – to keep them safe.

Tower of London

St Paul's burns

People had thought that St Paul's Cathedral would not burn, so they put their things there for safety when the fire started. Now St Paul's was full of books and paper, because there were many printers and booksellers nearby. Unfortunately, when the roof caught fire, melting lead from the roof set fire to things inside. Quickly, the cathedral was ablaze. The books and paper made it burn more fiercely.

Molten lead dripped from the roof on to the streets below.

John Evelyn reports from St Paul's

John Evelyn was a famous writer living in London at the time of the fire. Like Samuel Pepys, Evelyn kept a diary. He reported the awful scene: 'The stones of Paul's flew like grenados [hand grenades], the melting lead running down the streets in a stream, and the very pavements glowing with fiery redness, so as no horse, nor man, was able to tread on them.'

Gunpowder!

Meanwhile, Londoners had found a new and quick way of making wide firebreaks – they blew buildings up with gunpowder. Surrounded by wide firebreaks, the fire stopped spreading at last.

Gunpowder – scary but it worked!

Samuel Pepys noted that this new move of blowing houses up 'at first did frighten people more than anything, but it stopped the fire where it was done, bringing down the houses to the ground in the same places they stood, and then it was easy to quench what little fire [the explosion had started]'.

Samuel's firebreak works

At 2 a.m. on Wednesday, Samuel and his wife were sleeping in his office. Then they heard people shouting that the fire was near, and decided they should move out. Samuel came back to the office later that morning, having left his wife to guard their money. He found that the firebreak he had organized on Tuesday had worked. His house and office were not burned.

However, even as late as Wednesday, John Evelyn wrote that some people were still trying to stop the firebreaks, because they didn't want their houses to be blown up.

Wednesday 5 September

Things began to get better on Wednesday. The wind dropped. The fire stopped spreading so quickly, and sparks and cinders did not blow across the firebreaks to start new fires on the other side. Later on Wednesday, the fires began to go out, but some buildings were still on fire. The Clothworkers' Hall had cellars full of oil, which burned for three days. London was full of hot smouldering rubble – even six months later, Samuel Pepys wrote that he saw smoke coming from it. Smouldering things sometimes burst into flames, so there were some new small fires. But these were quickly put out.

London Bridge

The last few fires

Late on Wednesday, the roof of Middle Temple Hall caught fire. A sailor, Richard Rowe, and a soldier climbed up and put it out. Rowe was given ten pounds (equal to about a year's wages) as a reward. On Thursday, Samuel Pepys and some navy workers put out a new fire in Bishopsgate.

Plumes of smoke filled the sky even after the flames had been put out.

Tower of London

Thursday 6 September

Samuel from his office

Samuel spent the night of Thursday 6 September in his office. He wrote that he could see that the Clothworkers' Hall was still on fire and had burned for three days and nights because of the oil stored in the cellar.

Friday 7 September

John Evelyn burns his shoes

On Friday 7 September, John walked through the city to St Paul's 'with extraordinary difficulty, clambering over heaps of yet smoking rubbish, and frequently mistaking where I was; the ground under my feet so hot, that it even burnt the soles of my shoes'.

How bad was the damage?

About four-fifths of central London had been destroyed, but few Londoners had been killed by the flames. It is possible that some dead bodies were never found, but only four people were known to have died in the fire itself. One person was reported to have died of fright and several more were killed in collapsed houses. Perhaps seventy to eighty thousand Londoners were left homeless, and many had lost most of their possessions. The cost of the fire was thought to be £10 million. This was a huge amount of money and many times more than the entire annual income of London at that time. As a result, many people became destitute.

What was destroyed?

A survey made after the fire listed what was destroyed:

- 436 acres of London land
- 13,200 houses in 400 streets
- 87 churches (out of an original total of 109)
- 52 Livery Company halls (the official buildings that looked after the different tradespeople of London)
- The Royal Exchange, Guildhall – the offices of the Lord Mayor of London
- St Paul's Cathedral

The mood in the city

Londoners were confused, frightened and angry. Some thought the fire was a punishment from God. Others blamed foreigners, Catholics or other scapegoats. The king went to the refugee camps outside the city walls to tell people that the fire had been an accident, not an attack by foreign spies.

Invasion scares

John Evelyn tells us about a false rumour that said foreign troops had invaded. People in the refugee camps panicked and got ready to fight. Evelyn wrote: 'This report did so terrify, that . . . they ran from their goods, and, taking what weapons they could come at, they could not be stopped from [attacking any foreigners they met] without sense or reason.'

Angry scenes were common as many people feared being attacked.

Soldiers had to be sent to make the people go back to the camps again. People were nervous because yet more rumours told of foreign spies starting new fires. The people told Samuel Pepys that it was dangerous for strangers to be on the street.

Investigations and scapegoats

So how did the fire start? Parliament set up an inquiry to find out why the fire happened. The inquiry decided that the fire was an accident. This is almost certainly true.

Yet at a separate trial, French man Robert Hubert was found guilty and later executed for starting the fire. In 1681, the new Lord Mayor put up a plaque claiming the fire was the work of Catholics. (Those words were removed in 1830.)

Robert Hubert

Robert Hubert was a French watchmaker. He claimed that he had thrown a bomb into the Farriners' bakery to start the fire. But he kept changing his story: perhaps he was mentally ill, or was frightened into saying things. He probably was not even in London when the fire started. But he was found guilty all the same, and was executed on 27 October 1666.

Grand plans

Rebuilding London was a big job. Several people, including John Evelyn, drew up plans for rebuilding London in a very different way to before. But in the end these plans were all too expensive and too hard to organize. So mostly the city was rebuilt along the same street lines as before. But the buildings were very different – now they had to be made of brick or stone, and could not be so crowded together. These changes made another great fire less likely.

John Evelyn's plans

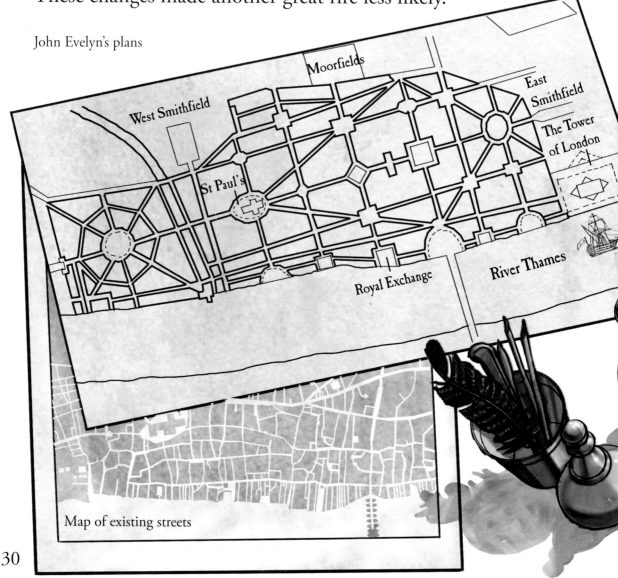

West Smithfield

Moorfields

East Smithfield

The Tower of London

St Paul's

Royal Exchange

River Thames

Map of existing streets

Christopher Wren

Christopher Wren was an architect who had already been working on St Paul's. He designed many public buildings that needed to be rebuilt after the fire, but his biggest project was the rebuilding of St Paul's Cathedral. He rebuilt fifty-one other churches, and other buildings, too.

Christopher Wren's plans

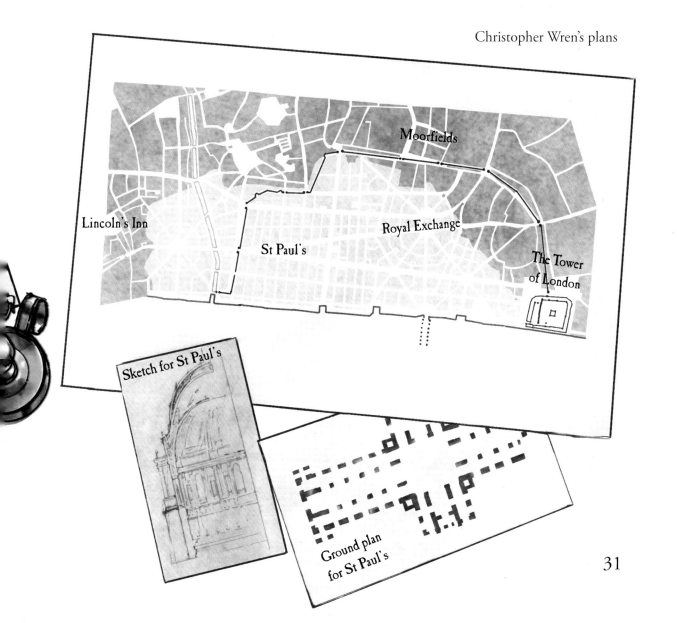

Moorfields

Lincoln's Inn

St Paul's

Royal Exchange

The Tower of London

Sketch for St Paul's

Ground plan for St Paul's

Rebuilding

Londoners began to rebuild their city. It took many months just to clear up the rubble and plan what to do next. By the end of 1667, only 150 new houses had been built. Then things speeded up: in 1668, 1,450 were built, with 2,000 new houses in 1669. Some buildings took longer to replace: the new St Paul's Cathedral was not completed until 1711.

It took many years to organize and complete the rebuilding of London.

Nightmares

Like many Londoners, Samuel was very shaken by the fire. On 15 September 1666, he wrote that he was; 'much terrified in the nights now-a-days with dreams of fire, and falling down of houses.' On 28 February 1667, he wrote: 'it is strange to think how to this very day I cannot sleep a-night without great terrors of fire.'

The Fire Court

People were worried that rebuilding the city would be delayed by arguments about who should pay for it. So a special court – the Fire Court – was set up to settle these arguments quickly and fairly. The Fire Court worked from 1667 to 1676.

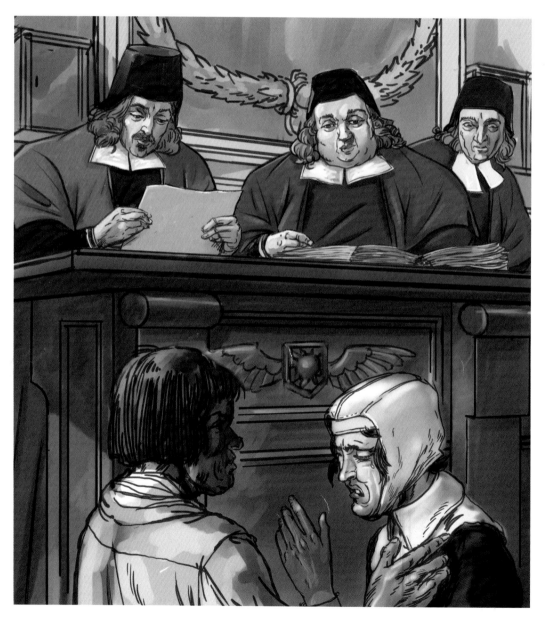

The Fire Court settled nearly 800 arguments in its first year.

Daniel Berry versus Sir George Waterman

Daniel Berry sold timber, but his warehouse on Cousin Lane had completely burned down in the fire. Daniel wanted to rebuild quickly and get back to work. But he rented his warehouse, and his landlord wanted to do something else with the site. The Fire Court heard the case in 1667 and helped Daniel and his landlord to agree what to do, and how much each should pay.

The Fire Court enabled Daniel to rebuild his warehouse and get back into business.

Fire brigades

One of the problems during the Great Fire was that most people had tried to save their own things, and they left firefighting to others. It wasn't clear enough whose job it was to fight big fires. To fix this problem, people began to set up organized fire brigades.

Nicholas Barbon

Nicholas Barbon set up one of the first fire brigades in 1680. Fire brigades were run by insurance companies. You paid money to the insurance company and, if your house caught fire, they sent their fire brigade to put the fire out. They would only do this if you had a sign on your house to say you had paid to insure it. It was not until 1866 that a public London Fire Brigade was formed, ready to put out any fire.

Fire-insurance sign

Teams of firefighters worked together to put the fires out.

Remembering the fire

A permanent memorial to the destruction caused by the fire was designed by Sir Christopher Wren. Called 'the Monument', it was built from Portland stone and took six years to complete. It still stands to this day. The monument is 62 metres (202 feet) high – its height in feet being the same as its distance from the site in Pudding Lane where the fire began. At the top is a gilt bronze vase of flames symbolizing the flames of the fire.

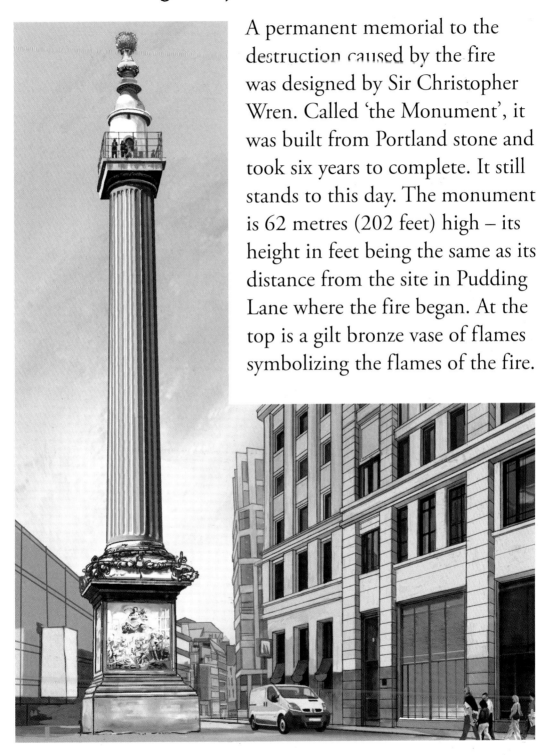

There are 311 steps inside the Monument leading to a viewing gallery.

Who's who?

Charles II (King) 1630–1685

Charles II was the eldest son of King Charles I (who was deposed and executed at the end of the English Civil War). Charles II invaded England with a Scottish army in 1651, but was defeated by Oliver Cromwell. In 1660, after Cromwell's death, Charles was invited to return to Britain and become king.

Christopher Wren 1632–1723

Christopher trained as a mathematician and astronomer, and became a Professor of Astronomy at Gresham College, London. In 1662 he helped set up the Royal Society, an organization for promoting science. He then became interested in designing buildings. His first designs were for Pembroke College Chapel and the Sheldonian Theatre in Oxford.

James, Duke of York 1633–1701

James was the younger brother of King Charles II. He became an admiral in the Royal Navy and fought at the Battle of Lowestoft, where he was nearly killed. He took charge of the firefighting efforts in the Great Fire, with great success. James became King James II after his brother King Charles II died, but he was forced from power in 1688.

John Evelyn 1620–1706

As a young man, John travelled around Italy and became a keen writer, gardener and book collector. He wrote a book about the problems of pollution in London, published in 1661– five years before the fire. He also kept a diary for several years, containing vivid accounts of the things he saw.

Nicholas Barbon 1640–1698

Nicholas was the eldest son of Praise-God Barbon, who had been a preacher and an MP in 'Barebone's Parliament', a parliament of men selected by Oliver Cromwell. Nicholas had the unusual middle name 'If-Jesus-Christ-Had-Not-Died-For-Thee-Thou-Hadst-Been-Damned'. Nicholas set up an insurance scheme that could send a fire brigade to put out fires in customers' houses.

Richard Rowe

Richard was a sailor. He climbed to the roof of the Middle Temple Hall when it caught fire and was able to put out the flames. He was given a ten-pound reward for this.

Robert Hubert c. 1640–1666

Robert was a French watchmaker, executed for starting the Great Fire of London. It is almost certain that he did not do this. Although he confessed to throwing a fire bomb into the Farriners' bakery, he kept changing his story. Later, a ship's captain remembered that Hubert was not even in London until two days after the fire started. Robert was hanged despite these doubts.

Samuel Pepys 1633–1703

Samuel was an official in the Royal Navy. He was in charge of an office that organized navy supplies. But he is best known because he kept a diary from 1660–69. Samuel's diary describes important historical events such as the Great Plague (1665) and the Great Fire (1666), but it also covers the events of his daily life.

Thomas Bloodworth (Lord Mayor of London) c. 1620–1682

Thomas Bloodworth, or (Bludworth), was Lord Mayor of London at the time of the Great Fire. Many people blamed him for not ordering houses to be pulled down just after the fire started. They thought that the fire could have been stopped from spreading if the mayor had given permission to make firebreaks sooner.

Thomas Farriner c. 1615–1670

Thomas and his daughter Hanna owned a bakery in Pudding Lane where the Great Fire started. Thomas is sometimes called 'the king's baker' because he made biscuits for the Royal Navy.

The Great Fire timeline

1660

• Charles II comes to the throne, restoring the monarchy after the English Civil War. His coronation is on 23 April 1661.

• Samuel Pepys begins keeping his diary.

1665

• Outbreak of plague in London. One in five Londoners dies, and city life is badly disrupted.

• The Second Dutch War. England and Holland are at war from 1665–67.

1666

• France declares war on England.

• 2–6 September: The Great Fire of London.

The Great Fire 1666

Sunday 2 September

• The fire starts about 1 a.m. in Pudding Lane.
• It quickly spreads, helped by a strong wind and delays in organizing firebreaks.
• By morning, around 300 houses have been destroyed.
• The fire spreads down towards London Bridge.
• It is difficult to organize enough firefighters.
• Many people are busy packing up their goods and moving them away from the fire. Other people are busy making money by charging high prices to rent the carts people need to carry off their things.
• Rumours start that the fire was caused by enemy agents. (England is at war with France and Holland in 1666.)

Monday 3 September

• The Duke of York takes charge of firefighting operations.
• The fire is visible from Oxford (around 100 km away).
• Refugees begin to gather in open spaces near London.
• Mobs attack foreigners, wrongly thinking that they are starting fires.

Tuesday 4 September

• The wind is still strong and blows the fire across the Duke of York's firebreaks.
• St Paul's Cathedral is completely destroyed.

Wednesday 5 September

• The wind drops, and the fire is slowly brought under control.
• Samuel Pepys, John Evelyn and other writers record vivid memories of the smouldering rubble and refugee camps.
• A new fire at Temple is quickly put out by Richard Rowe.

Thursday 6 September

• Early on Thursday morning a new fire at Bishopsgate starts, but it is quickly put out. The Great Fire is over.
• King Charles II addresses the crowd to say that the fire was an accident.

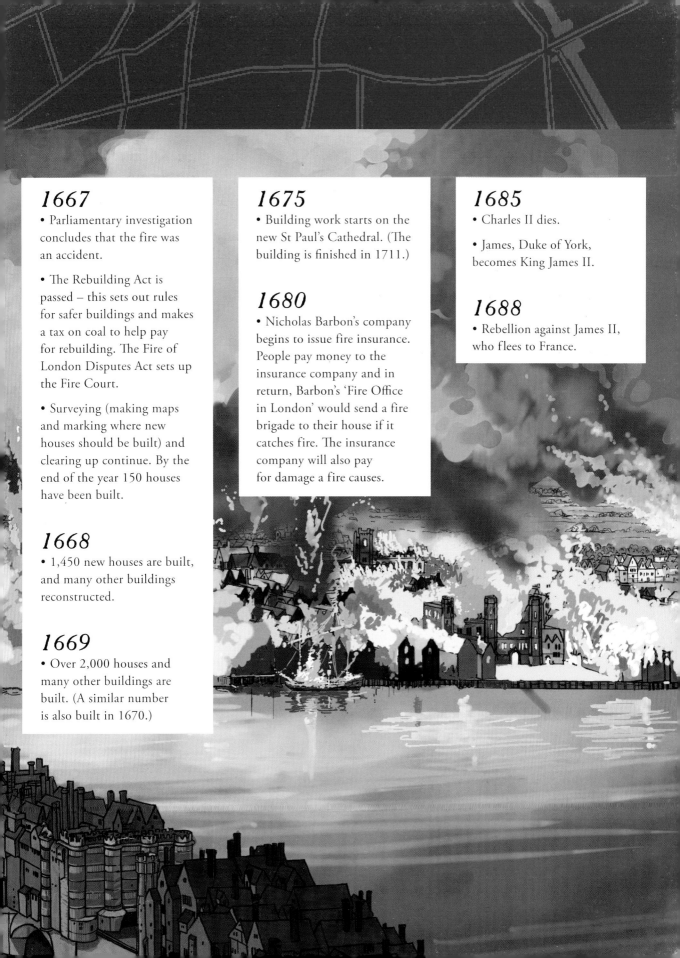

1667

• Parliamentary investigation concludes that the fire was an accident.

• The Rebuilding Act is passed – this sets out rules for safer buildings and makes a tax on coal to help pay for rebuilding. The Fire of London Disputes Act sets up the Fire Court.

• Surveying (making maps and marking where new houses should be built) and clearing up continue. By the end of the year 150 houses have been built.

1668

• 1,450 new houses are built, and many other buildings reconstructed.

1669

• Over 2,000 houses and many other buildings are built. (A similar number is also built in 1670.)

1675

• Building work starts on the new St Paul's Cathedral. (The building is finished in 1711.)

1680

• Nicholas Barbon's company begins to issue fire insurance. People pay money to the insurance company and in return, Barbon's 'Fire Office in London' would send a fire brigade to their house if it catches fire. The insurance company will also pay for damage a fire causes.

1685

• Charles II dies.

• James, Duke of York, becomes King James II.

1688

• Rebellion against James II, who flees to France.

Pudding Lane bakery biscuits

Some reports say that the fire started when small cakes caught fire in the bakery's oven. Try this recipe for traditional biscuits.

You will need:

A mixing bowl
A spoon
A sieve
A greased baking tray
Oven gloves
Sugar for sprinkling

Ingredients:

(makes 24 biscuits)
225g softened butter
110g caster sugar
275g plain flour
75g currants
1 teaspoon mixed spice

Share them with friends!

Ask an adult to preheat the oven to 180°C / gas mark 4. Beat the butter and sugar together in a mixing bowl until they are smooth.

Sift the flour and mixed spice into the bowl, add the currants and mix into a dough. Mould the dough into a ball.

Lightly dust your work surface with flour and roll the dough into small balls with your hands. Use your hands to flatten the balls into biscuit shapes.

Place the biscuits on a baking tray and bake for 15–20 minutes, until golden brown. Ask an adult to help you with the oven. Sprinkle the biscuits with sugar. Leave to cool.

Make a London house

You will need

a photocopier
scissors
colouring pencils
double-sided tape
or a glue stick

Instructions

· Photocopy these pages.
· Colour the lower and upper parts of the house with a timber pattern. Colour the roof with a tiled pattern.
· Cut out each part.

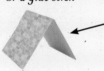

The roof
Fold the roof in half along the dotted line. Stick it to the tabs of the assembled upper house.

Upper house
Fold along the dotted lines and stick down the side tabs to make the upper box. Fold in the tabs for the roof.

Lower house
Fold along the dotted lines and stick down the tabs to make a box. Stick the upper house to the lower house.

The roof

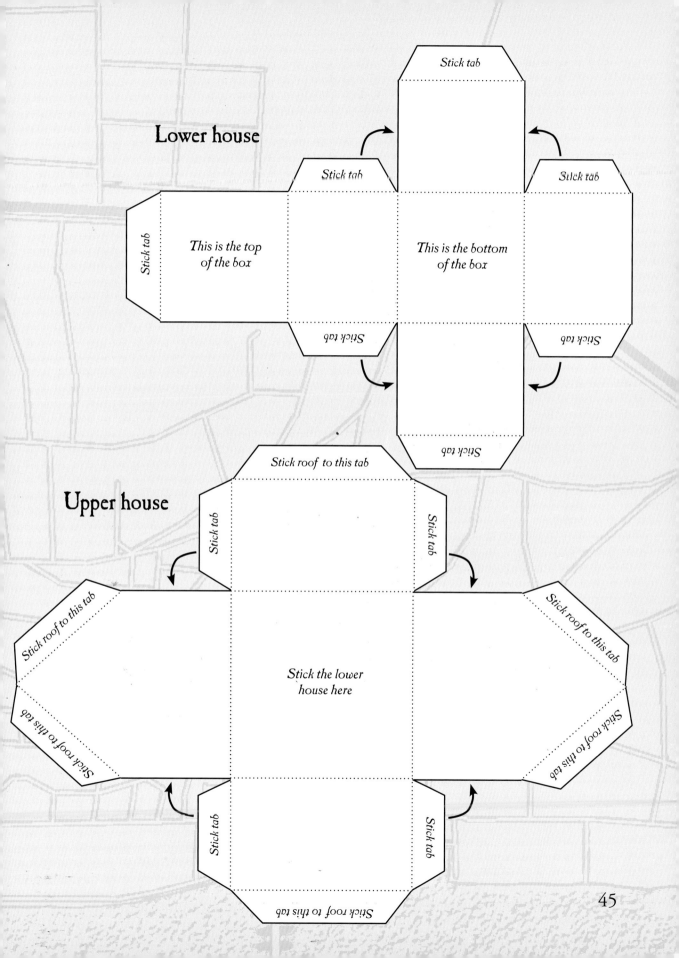

Lower house

Stick tab

Stick tab

Stick tab

Stick tab

This is the top of the box

This is the bottom of the box

Stick tab

Stick tab

Stick tab

Stick roof to this tab

Upper house

Stick tab

Stick tab

Stick roof to this tab

Stick roof to this tab

Stick roof to this tab

Stick roof to this tab

Stick the lower house here

Stick tab

Stick tab

Stick roof to this tab

45

Great Fire word search

Find the words listed below and circle them on the grid.

ASH   MONUMENT   SMOULDER

DAMAGE   PUDDING LANE   THAMES

FIREBREAK   SAMUEL PEPYS   WATER

HEAT   SMOKE   WIND

A	S	H	C	D	S	M	O	U	L	D	E	R
V	A	E	R	S	Y	O	E	M	E	W	T	P
S	M	O	K	E	N	N	L	E	B	X	E	W
Q	U	T	Y	R	O	U	Q	N	T	S	F	J
I	E	C	T	H	A	M	E	S	Q	Y	I	P
U	L	K	P	Y	I	E	W	O	C	P	R	A
G	P	U	D	D	I	N	G	L	A	N	E	E
D	E	R	A	U	F	T	F	P	R	H	B	S
W	P	I	M	L	G	P	W	A	T	E	R	B
Z	Y	P	A	B	H	O	I	Q	F	I	E	F
P	S	W	G	A	B	Q	N	E	H	E	A	T
N	R	C	E	Q	C	V	D	R	M	A	K	I

Glossary

destitute very poor and having nothing (many people lost everything they had in the Great Fire)

Fire Court a court set up to sort out disagreements between people who were arguing about how to rebuild and who should pay for it

firebreak a gap made between houses to stop the fire spreading from one building to the next

fire-insurance sign a sign fixed to a building to prove that the owner had paid for fire insurance

guild an organization set up to look after the needs of workers in a particular trade, such as bakers or weavers

Monument the memorial to the Great Fire, 62 metres (202 feet) from Pudding Lane

refugee camp a camp for people forced leave their homes

scapegoat someone who is blamed for something they did not do

squirt a piece of early firefighting equipment, like a giant water pistol

Index